SO-BRC-516

With the kind regards

of William Lawrence.

Bishop of

Massachusetts.

1903 -

PHILLIPS BROOKS

A Study

PHILLIPS BROOKS

A Study

BY

WILLIAM LAWRENCE, D.D.

BISHOP OF MASSACHUSETTS

BOSTON AND NEW YORK
HOUGHTON, MIFFLIN AND COMPANY
The Riverside Press, Cambridge
1903

NOTE

Oɴ the twenty-third day of January, 1903, was observed the tenth anniversary of the death of Phillips Brooks.

The Dioceses of Massachusetts and Western Massachusetts, over which, as one diocese, he had presided as Bishop, joined in a service of commemoration in Trinity Church, Boston.

The multitude which gathered, crowding the church to the doors, the long procession of bishops and clergy, the presence of many other ministers and of representative citizens, bore witness to his living power and to the loyalty of the people to his memory.

The address given at that service is in the following pages, published, with a few verbal changes since its delivery, at the request of the Standing Committee of the Diocese of Massachusetts.

With all other interpreters of Phillips Brooks, I am under obligations to the Rev. Dr. A. V. G. Allen.

WILLIAM LAWRENCE.

BOSTON, February 12, 1903.

PHILLIPS BROOKS

PHILLIPS BROOKS

TIME adjusts our vision and en-
ables us to study men in new
relations.   The distant figure is often
in better perspective and takes on
truer proportions.   The passage of
even ten years throws into the background many features once conspicu-
ous, and reveals other deeper charac-
teristics.

With the rapid movement of life
in these days, it is very seldom that
at the end of ten years from his death
a man is thus commemorated.   This
very fact suggests one rare feature in
the character of Phillips Brooks, that

of calling forth the best emotions and grateful sentiments.

To many of you present in this church, which is so associated with him, his personal presence is vivid. His majestic figure in this pulpit, the action of his body, the tones of his voice, the animation of his face, and the glow of his imagery all come back as if it were yesterday. Some of you would prefer silence, that you might recall precious memories and gather from the past treasures of sympathetic words and hopeful messages, which you feel are peculiarly your own. You would like simply to thank God for the gift of his life, enter again into communion with him through Christ, and go quietly home. There was that about his personality, a divine possession, which kindled the faith of those who came in contact with him; there was some subtle power in his companionship which those who have read his works, but who never met him, can never realize.

There are others here, and many throughout the land, who, never having seen or heard him, have through his printed sermons reached deep into his thought and his interpretations of Christ, and who thank God for his message to them. He had no ambition to add to the religious literature of the day. When, however, one realizes that over two hundred thousand volumes of his sermons and other writings are in the hands of the people and that many hundreds of thousands of his messages of all kinds are scattered throughout the homes and libraries of America and England, one catches a suggestion of the breadth and depth of his influence and of the gratitude of the people for his life. There is an ambition higher than that of the creation of so-called permanent literature : it is that of making a contribution towards the spiritual wealth of the people, the kindling of high ideals, and the increase of the power of Christ. Such spiritual power entering into man and transmitted to others is permanent.

If the passage of these short ten years has enabled us to study Phillips Brooks in better perspective, may it not be well to place on record some of the results of the study? This, therefore, is what I ask of you, that in the light of these ten years we consider some of the deeper elements in the life and thought of Phillips Brooks, — elements that had such power twenty and thirty years ago as evidently to affect the life and thought of to-day.

No true friend of his would claim that he was the only representative of these elements, or that he was always the leader. Some of the conditions and powers were in the intellectual and spiritual atmosphere, and his was a sensitive organization. With all this said, however, it is clear that he was one of the prophets of his time; he spoke for God; there were occasions when he stood on mountain tops and when his spiritual vision swept a horizon wider than that of his brethren. He was an interpreter of the truth to the spiritual experiences of men; he was a leader among those even who marched in the van ; and his leadership was greatest in the strength, simplicity, and beauty of his own character.

In the first half of the nineteenth century, and even into the second half, there was no conception of the unity of the universe. As the stars were aloft and separate from all relations to the world, so to a great degree was God from man. The natural man had nothing in common with the spiritual man; there were two classes of men — the sinners and the saints. The two natures of Christ were not only sharply defined and fixed, but even separated, as in the effort to determine what he did and said as God and what he did and said as man. The Atonement was a transaction as separate from man as the proceedings of a judicial court are from the people. Theology had as little relation to life as dogma had to ethics. The members of the Church were the elect; all others were given over to the uncovenanted mercies of God. Under these conditions Phillips Brooks was educated, although the rich piety and sympathy of his home tempered somewhat the rigor of contemporary thought.

In the very texture of his life, inwrought through generations of prayer and piety, was faith in God. From childhood he lived in the very presence of God; pure in life, rich in imagination, throbbing with spiritual aspirations, he brooded over the problems of God, the Atonement, and the relation of Christ to his Father and to man.

His conception of an infinite, loving, heavenly Father, a merciful Saviour, and a world of men, women, and little children would not adjust itself to the prevailing theology. He recognized in the break of the liberals from the old standards a healthy reaction, and he sympathized with much in it: but that did not for him meet the situation; there was something provincial, limited, and sectarian about it all. He held back from close relations to the Church, and sustained a deep reserve on religious questions. German thought was as yet unknown to him. As he was brooding and searching among the libraries, Coleridge and Wordsworth fell into his hands; then Maurice and Tennyson, Bacon and the ancient philosopher Philo, Bushnell and Robertson. With one and another of these his poetic instincts were aroused; his imagination leaped at the revelations, and there opened to him a new heaven and a new earth, bound together, interwoven by the eternal principles of God's love and righteousness. His possession of these truths was not so much by the reason as by the spiritual apprehension of the whole man : he laid hold of them, reveled in them, dreamed them, and lived them. He had worshipped God and prayed to God, — now he discovered that he

was living in God. The world had
seemed to be the reality, and God
the distant spirit. Now God was to
him the only reality; the spirit was
life, and Nature with all her beauty
was the radiant expression of God's
glory. The whole universe was the
living, throbbing expression of his
power and love; all were bound together in a common purpose, with
God as their centre. The world was
not Satan's, but God's; it was his
from the beginning.

His spiritual sympathies turned to
man's relation to God. The theology
of Calvinism ran in his blood. He
faced the problems, Was man the
child of Satan, or of God? Was
man by nature given over to sin only
to become God's child by some pro-

cess of conversion or the acceptance
of some theory of the Atonement ?
The answers came to him clearer
and clearer as his thought matured.
Man was by his very birth the child
of God; sin was the intruder.   Men
through their sin estranged themselves from the Father, as did the
prodigal ; therein were the horror
and punishment of sin.   But in his
very nature man was from God, made
in his image, akin to his substance
or nature.   The eternal fatherhood of
God was the burden of his preaching.
From the beginning Christ Jesus was
of God and with God — very man,
very God.   From the very essence of
his loving fatherhood, God sent forth
his Son, who took upon himself the
form of man and lived among men.

It was the oneness of the spiritual nature of man with God that enabled each to know the other. "We talk about men's reaching through Nature up to Nature's God. It is nothing to the way in which they may reach through manhood up to manhood's God and learn the divine love by the human."[1] "A brute race could have seen no Incarnation. . . . 'Because we are sons, God hath sent forth the spirit of his Son into our hearts.' Because we are sons, his Son himself could take our nature upon him."[2]

"I am the light of the world — a thousand subtle, mystic miracles of deep and intricate relationship between Christ and humanity must be

[1] *Sermons*, vol. v. p. 51.
[2] *Ib.*, vol. i. p. 240.

enfolded in these words; but over and behind and within all other meanings, it means this : the essential richness and possibility of humanity and its essential belonging to divinity." [1]

The truth of the Incarnation was the central truth of his life, thought, and preaching. For him it solved the pressing problems of life and nature, and knit the universe, God, and his creation into living unity.

It was this fundamental truth, bound up as it is in the fact of the divine sonship of man, that led him to his belief in the value of the human soul, which, you remember, marked the climax of his Lectures on Preaching. With the movement of science the individual was losing

[1] *Sermons*, vol. v. p. 4.

his value. Phillips Brooks threw himself just then into that breach with all his power, and affirmed the essential value of the individual. This gave him the evangelical element in his message ; this emphasized the direct responsibility of each soul to God, and enabled him while preaching to the larger world to bring his words home to the conscience and aspirations of each man, woman, and child within sound of his voice.

It was this, too, that made him a source of inspiration to all workers in the uplifting of the down-trodden. He had very little interest in preaching upon the methods and work of social service, deeply as he was interested in those who were carrying them out. His mission was to reach the deeper motives and strike the springs of enthusiasm, not so much for humanity in the abstract as for men, God's children; and through his preaching the springs gushed forth.

He had an unwavering belief in the presence of the Holy Spirit brooding over, guiding, and energizing in the midst of men and of Christ's Church. The Spirit was in the world to-day as really and as evidently as at Pentecost or in the Middle Ages. The Spirit was revealing truth from every source of thought and life. He was the Spirit of Truth. Hence Phillips Brooks had unbounded confidence in the Church, if only she would keep ear and heart open to the voice and influence of the Spirit. Thus he was led to his faith in the Trinity, not as the description of God (for what mortal can describe God?), but as the description of what we know of God. " I should," he said, " count any Sunday's work unfitly done in which the Trinity was not the burden of our preaching. For when we preach the fatherhood of God, we preach his divinity; when we point to Christ, the perfect Saviour, it is a divine Redeemer that we declare; and when we plead with men to hear the voice and yield to the persuasions of the Holy Spirit, the Comforter, into whose comfort we invite them, is divine. The divinity of Father, Son, and Holy Ghost, this is our gospel. By this gospel we look for salvation. It is a gospel to be used, to be believed in, and to be lived by; not merely to be kept and admired and discussed and explained." [1]

Believing as he did in God, and in all men as the children of God, he always had before him the ideal manhood, the ideal church.   He broke away from the conception of the Church as a body of men separate, set apart from their fellows as the religious and the saved, the body of the elect.   On the contrary, " The Church is no exception and afterthought in the world, but is the survival and preservation of the world's first idea, — the anticipation and prophecy of the world's final perfectness.   The Church of Christ is the ideal humanity.   Say not that it leaves out the superhuman.   I know no ideal hu-

[1] *Sermons,* vol. i. p. 228.

manity that is not filled and pervaded
with the superhuman. God in man
is not unnatural, but the absolutely
natural. That is what the Incarnation makes us know." [1]

The sacraments of the Church are
therefore the symbols of the recognition of the fact that each child is a
child of God and hence a member
of his church, and also of the contin-
ual gift of Christ to those who feed
on him and his strengthening power.
"The unity of his believers to the
end of time is still to have the secret
of its existence in the personal relation between each of them and him.
To help this invisible relation to realize itself and not to be all lost in the
unseen, the gracious kindness of the

[1] Quoted in the *Life*, vol. ii. p. 659.

Master provides two symbols which
thenceforth become the pledges at
once of the personal believer's belonging to the Lord and of the belonging of believers to each other.
The sacraments are set like gems to
hold the Church into its precious
unity." [1] Those of you who have
witnessed the baptism of an infant by
him, who have perhaps followed him
to the cradle of a dying child, recall the tenderness of his voice, the
deep emotion and the reality of the
rite. Beneath the words sounded the
note of deep conviction and love. It
was no defense of an empty rite but
the conviction of a vital truth that
prompted his words upon the baptism
of a dying child : "Baptism is the

[1] *Sermons,* vol. v. p. 179.

solemn, grateful, tender recognition, during the brief moments of that infant's life on earth, of the deep meanings of his humanity. It is the human race in its profoundest self-consciousness welcoming this new member to its multitude. Only for a few moments does he tarry in this condition of humanity; his life touches the earth only to leave it; but in those few moments of his tarrying, humanity lifts up its hand and claims him, . . . appropriates for him that redemption of Christ which revealed man's belonging to God, declares him a member of that church which is simply humanity, as belonging to God." [1]

The Lord's Supper was to Phillips

[1] *Sermons,* vol. iv. pp. 43 and 44.

Brooks the great high feast of Christ, the Head of humanity. It belonged, then, not to any one body of Christians; no single denomination had a right to restrict it; it belonged ideally to all humanity and practically to every man who claimed Christ as his Master and Saviour, and who tried to live in Christ's spirit. Each denomination held it in trust for Christ and his followers. Hence his welcome, given never in his own name, but in accordance with what he believed to be the law as well as the spirit of his church, to all Christian people to partake of its blessings.

Whether Christ himself appointed three orders of the ministry was to him of little moment as compared with the great truth that in the unfolding of the life of the Church the ministry had evolved through the guidance and power of the Holy Spirit and under the leadership of Christ. To him the ministry was therefore divinely ordered and guided.

In this short and very imperfect sketch of the deeper features of his faith I may have seemed to try to do what Phillips Brooks always claimed was impossible, — disentangle a man's faith, beliefs, and aspirations from the other elements of his life. Such, of course, has not been my purpose. His beliefs were interwoven with the very texture of his whole life and character. There was no scrap of his creed that did not have its vital relation with his life, and no little act of each day that did not have its vital relation with some of the deepest truths of his faith.

This, then, is what I have been trying to set forth as the first great contribution of Phillips Brooks to the religious thought of his day. First, the realization of the unity of the universe — God, man, and nature inextricably interwoven, spiritual and material, a living organism, working out God's purpose. And bound up in the first, the unity of man, divine and human, spiritual and physical, the indissolubility of his personality.

Those who are young and who have been educated in these thoughts can have no conception of the relief, light, and exhilaration that they brought to the past generation; they were the dispelling of darkness by the light of the

rising sun.   The scriptures took on a
new meaning; the thought of how the
whole creation groaned and travailed
until the coming of Christ was a reve-
lation; the sympathy of nature and
man in the Incarnation touched the
hearts of children, and ten thousand
of them caught up his carol and burst
into song: —

> " For Christ is born of Mary,
>   And gathered all above,
>   While mortals sleep, the angels keep
>   Their watch of wondering love.
>   O Morning Stars, together
>   Proclaim the holy birth!
>   And praises sing to God the King
>   And peace to men on earth."

Such a conception of the unity of
God's universe may sometimes seem
to touch the borders of pantheism;

error is but the over-emphasis of truth. The Christian faith has, however, always been safeguarded by the conception of personality, the personality of God and of man.

You recall the emphasis of Phillips Brooks upon the vital worth of personality in the preacher : " Preaching is the communication of truth by man to men.   It has in it two essential elements, truth and personality. . . . However the gospel may be capable of statement in dogmatic form, its truest statement is not in dogma but in personal life.   Christianity is Christ." [1]

It was this truth of the unity of man's personality that gave to the people of his day a new and more Christian conception of the relation of man

[1] *Lectures on Preaching*, pp. 5 and 7.

to death and to the life to come.   There
was aroused in all who heard him a
new sense of the dignity and the responsibility of manhood and a serene
confidence in God's regard for man.

Through this truth we are brought
naturally to the second contribution
of Phillips Brooks to the thought and
life of his day; it sounds common-
place now, almost unworthy of mention, so thoroughly has it become a
part of the texture of our life.   I
mean his complete confidence in God
as the God of truth, and in Christ as
indeed the Truth.

Some of you have no conception
of the dread that from time to time
was felt by Christian people at the
discovery of truths which might be
antagonistic to the Christian faith.

When some new and bold statement
of science was made, almost the whole
Christian world shuddered at its possible result.   It was a time, many
thought, for the strengthening of the
old defenses.   The recent death of
Archbishop Temple has reminded us
of the extreme sensitiveness of the
Church at the publication of the " Essays and Reviews."   Frankly, there
was a latent and very deep spirit of
scepticism in the Church, which dis-
trusted the truth, and which mistrusted
as to whether the fundamental belief
in God and Christ were the truth.
The dominating spirit of the nineteenth century, the restless search for
truth, continued to rise, however, and
the two forces were bound to meet.
Young men were looking for lead-

ers, for prophets who were above the
smoke of the battle.   Among others,
and, for some of us, above others, was
heard the voice of Phillips Brooks.
His message was that God is truth
and righteousness and love.   Whatever truth is discovered, and from
whatever source revealed, it is of God.
Man must keep mind and heart ever
open to new revelations of God.   He
had little sympathy with the efforts so
to interpret the truths of science as to
patch up and adjust the scriptures and
articles of faith from time to time.   He
had too much confidence in the essential spiritual truths beneath the statements of the faith of the Church.   He
had no patience with that man or
church who was timidly asking of
present thought, " Is it orthodox ? "

The vital question was, "Is it true?"[1]
And as Christ is Light, the Church
and men cannot hide behind dog-
mas and tradition, but must come
forth and speak and reason in the
light.   His own verse reveals his attitude : —

" Truth keeps no secret pensioners; whoe'er
Eats of her bread must wear her livery too,
Her temple must be built where men can see;
And when the worshipper comes up to it,
It must be in broad noonlight, singing psalms
And bearing offerings, that the world may know
Whose votaries they are and whom they praise."[2]

Having, therefore, this complete
confidence in the truth, and living in
communion with the God of truth,

[1] *Essays and Addresses*, p. 196.
[2] *Life*, vol. i. p. 243.

fired as he was with the love of God
and of men, he was impelled to preach
and speak with all the abandonment
of a man who is clear as to his cause,
and the end of the battle, but perfectly regardless of the present results
either to himself or to his fellows.
It was this that gave him that positive and assertive power. Men com-
plained that he did not reason with
cool logic, but that he swept them
along with him by the power of his
conviction and his personality. It is
true; for highly as he esteemed the
reason, he always felt that other qualities entered into the discussion of
truth — moral and spiritual qualities;
and because of his possession of these
he made them the reinforcement of
his argument. This confidence in God

as the God of truth was also the secret of what some felt to be his dan-
ger, — that of entering into the camp
of the enemy.   He had nothing of the
latent scepticism and timidity which
feel that truth must necessarily be
contaminated by contact with error
or that Christ is compromised by the
recognition of truth embedded in error.   He had such confidence in his
own faith in Christ that he had no
hesitation in recognizing, ay, rather
welcoming gladly, any ray of truth
from whatever source it came.   He
believed so firmly in his Church, too,
her creeds and standards, that he was
confident that she would with him
welcome truth from the agnostic, the
Calvinist, the Unitarian, or any other
sincere truth - seeker.   To speak in

glowing eloquence of the character
and the personal faith of James Free-
man Clarke, a Unitarian and one of
the spiritual leaders of Boston, was
the most natural thing in the world.
It never occurred to him that in so
speaking he would be held respon-
sible for the theology of Dr. Clarke,
from certain features of which he dif-
fered fundamentally.   His object was
the glad recognition by the Church
of a character full of love, purity, and
self-sacrifice, and by such recognition
he believed that the Church is always
the richer.

It was, too, this complete confidence in the God of truth that made
him the interpreter and the exemplar
of tolerance.   Through life he thought
much over the bigotry of some of the

champions of the faith, of their perse-
cution of the seekers for truth, and of
the nerveless quality of some of those
who were called most tolerant in his
day.   There was a feeling abroad that
depth and strength of religious conviction necessarily created a spirit of
intolerance, and that the true road to
charity was through the broad path of
indifference to truth and creed.

His studies of the character of
Christ had shown him how mistaken
this assumption was, for no one was
ever more convinced of the truth or
more positive in his statements of his
faith than was Jesus, and none ever
lived so tolerant of the sincere convictions of others.   As was his habit,
Phillips Brooks took the position not
of defense but of offense.   The two

essentials of a tolerant spirit were, as he put them, " first, positive conviction; and, second, sympathy with men whose convictions differ from our own." [1]   " We want to assert most positively that, so far from earnest personal conviction and generous tolerance being incompatible with one another, the two are necessary each to each." [2]   With him, however, no discussion reached its true plane until it had struck the level of personality and religion.   " True tolerance consists in the love of truth and the love of man, each brought to its perfection, and living in perfect harmony with one another; but these two great affections are perfect and in perfect harmony only when they are

[1] *Tolerance*, p. 7.   [2] *Ib.* p. 9.

orbed and enfolded in the yet greater
affection of the love of God." [1] "I
have tried to show not merely that a
man may be cordially tolerant and yet
devoutly spiritual, but also that a man
cannot attain to the highest tolerance
without being devoutly spiritual." [2]
"The hope of tolerance lies in the ad-
vancing spirituality of man." [3] "We
may adjust relations as we will; we
may decide just how far we can coöp-
erate with this or that heretic. . . . It
is all surface work. . . . Only a deeper
vitality, a richer filling of our spirits
with the spirit of God; an assurance
of the possible divineness of the human life by an experience of how
richly it may be filled with divinity, —

[1] *Ib*. p. 25.   [2] *Ib*. pp. 46 and 47.
[3] *Ib*. p. 57.

only this can make us be to our brethren and make them be to us all that
God designed." [1]

It was this same confidence in God,
the truth, that kept him serene during
the apparent victories of doubt and
scepticism.   Throughout his active
life in the ministry, the attitude of
the Christian world towards nature, the
scriptures, and man was revolution-
ized; even now our memories and
imaginations can scarcely grasp the
change.   Phillips Brooks stood to
many as the leading interpreter of
evangelical truth; hundreds of people
who felt themselves sinking into un-
belief turned to him with the despera-
tion of drowning men.   All this time
his attitude was changing, he was

[1] *Ib*. pp. 109 and 110.

thinking and living his faith out to its conclusion; nevertheless, so firm was his hold upon the deeper spiritual truths, so strong his grasp upon God, so close his sympathy with Christ, that he guided and, in spite of himself, even carried others while he moved also himself; and always unruffled, serene, and full of hope. For if God is the truth, then whatever the present troubles, the truth will be revealed and will prevail. The man of God must be a man of hope.

So in their sorrows and losses he became to the people the interpreter of the God of comfort. Never weak, always positive, he led the mourner away from self to higher thoughts and larger responsibilities.

Another contribution of Phillips

Brooks was the emphasis of the natu-
ralness and healthiness of the religious
life. We need not recall the theology
of the last century, the natural man at
enmity with God, children by the fact
of their birth shut out of the kingdom,
religion a supplement to life, artificial,
conventional, the fabrication of adult
morbid brains. We need not remind
ourselves either that the truth of man's
divine sonship had already begun to
be preached in some quarters. It was
the work of Phillips Brooks to take
that truth of man's divine sonship,
therefore man's simple natural instinct
for God, of the religious man, as the
most manly, most human man — up-
lift it before the people, iterate and
reiterate it until even the dullest could
comprehend, while the more spiritual

leaped and embraced it as one of the revelations that they had longed for. His work was to bring before men the typical man, Christ Jesus; for his was the simplest, most natural, most healthy life, because from beginning to end it dwelt in God. That the subject of his first sermon should be "The Simplicity that is in Christ" was an almost foregone conclusion. The motive of the Christian was of the simplest: "Religion is the life of man in gratitude and obedience and consequent growing likeness to Jesus Christ."[1] How familiar it all sounds to us now! It was new and fresh then. "Christianity seeks not to cramp man's nature, saying to him constantly 'Thou shalt not,' but it leads on, up to

[1] *Essays and Addresses*, p. 40.

freer air and wider space, wherein the soul may disport itself. It is God we follow; obeying God is freedom."[1] His appeal was constant for the simple, natural, richer life. "Pray for and work for fullness of life above everything; full red blood in the body; full honesty and truth in the mind, and the fullness of a grateful love for the Saviour in your heart."[2]

We can clearly see how this truth led up to his conception of sainthood, so different from that which has often prevailed in the Church, so different from that which was in the Church when he began to preach. "The spiritual life of man in its fullest sense is the activity of man's whole nature un-

[1] Address at Johns Hopkins University.
[2] *Life*, vol. ii. p. 178.

der the highest spiritual impulse, viz.,
the love of God."[1]   Men of strength
and power, not nerveless and effemi-
nate creatures, are the true types of
saintliness.   "I would present true
sainthood to you as the strong chain of
God's presence in humanity, running
down through all history, and making of it a unity, giving it a large and
massive strength able to bear great
things and to do great things too."[2]

Phillips Brooks was a prophet of
God, a preacher of Christ to men. He
is claimed, and by right, as the spiritual guide of people of all churches
and of no church.   His message and
influence passed over all denomina-
tional boundaries.   Thousands out-

[1] *Essays and Addresses,* p. 21.
[2] *Sermons,* vol. i. p. 177.

side of his own church looked to him
as their religious interpreter and pas-
tor, and he gratefully accepted the
fact.   He had, as we have seen, very
little interest in efforts for Christian
unity by adjustments or ecclesiastical
treaties and alliances.   His whole temper and his faith in the reality of spiritual powers compelled him to empha-
size the unity of the spirit.   "No," he
said, "the real unity of Christendom
is not to be found at last in identity
of organization, nor in identity of
dogma.   Both of those have been
dreamed of, and have failed; but in
the unity of spiritual consecration to
a common Lord."[1]   No one church,
therefore, can claim him as exclu-
sively hers.   He belonged to the

[1] *Tolerance*, p. 55.

Christian world of the nineteenth century.

To say, however, that he was in-
different as to ecclesiastical relations
and that his hold upon his own
church was simply one of accident
is to do him injustice and to misun-
derstand his whole conception of the
Church; for he believed that it was
only by standing where one is, by
certitude and conviction, that one can
really sympathize with and understand others.   It is only the loyal pa-
triot who can understand the patriot-
ism of other peoples; it is only the
faithful Christian of firm conviction
who can have true tolerance for the
sincere beliefs of the heathen; it is only
the loyal churchman who can really
and intelligently sympathize with the

earnest members of other churches and with those who claim no church. His quickness and frankness in pointing out the weaknesses in his own church arose, as he himself said again and again, from a deep sense of loyalty to her; the friend who cannot be frank with his friend is no true friend. And he had that confidence in the Church which assured him that she would gratefully welcome the sympathetic and honest correction.

He was at home in his church. He was perfectly conscious that he could be at home in no other. His whole temperament, his grasp of the historic significance of the Church, his conceptions of the Christian life and religious culture, his sense of proportion and of spiritual unity, his love of order, his conservative instincts, his artistic and poetic temperament, were satisfied in the Episcopal Church. To him a church with elaborate creeds was a house of bondage, and a church without creed was unthinkable; he demanded a creed so fundamental and so simple that in the stress of history it could hold the Church to the deep truths of the faith and at the same time could be continually filled with fresh spiritual thought and interpreted by new revelations of the truth. People who did not know or understand him sometimes said that he was restive in the Church and unsympathetic with its life. There were times when he was restive under certain limited conceptions of the Church, and he was occasionally unsympathetic with certain popular features of what are sometimes called churchly thought and habits; but he never had any other thought than that in the Church he was happy and at home. Of course he was there by right, and his loyalty to her and to what he firmly believed were her historic principles never wavered.

To those ministers, laymen, and theological students who turned to him with their doubts as to whether they had a right to remain in the Church, and who quoted the language of this or that churchman of the day, his unfailing answer was, "Why do you listen to him? No one man or group of men is the authoritative interpreter of the Church's standards. Look to your Prayer Book; what do

you find there ? Study it, interpret
it by the history of the Church, and
then and not till then make your deci-
sion." No churchman of his generation had a deeper, more intelligent,
more loyal devotion to the Prayer
Book than Phillips Brooks. It was
to him as were the scriptures, not a
book of legal bondage, but of spiritual liberty.

That his influence among Christian
people of all names was enhanced by
the fact that he was in the ministry of
the Episcopal Church, and of no other
body, is evident. For that position
gave him a standing ground well apart
and disassociated from the theological
differences of New England. He was
saturated with New England's theological thought, and could interpret

Protestant America to herself; at the same time, his official position associated him with what was finest in the history of English-speaking peoples.

It was only natural, therefore, that he who represented in so noble a way the highest traditions of the Church in England, and in his own country, should be consecrated a bishop. The wonder to us now is that any one should have thought differently. It is not strange, however, that his position should have been misunderstood by some; that is usually the lot of great men. And there are always those who are not conscious of the Church's historic comprehension of different types of thought. Looking back now, however, we see how nat-

urally he takes his place in the line
of great bishops who have enriched
the historic life of the Church.

One more feature in the character of Phillips Brooks I mention, and
with some hesitation, for it can best
be illustrated by a leaf from my experience as his successor in the episcopate.

When it became my duty to follow
him in the visitation of the churches,
I found, of course, a deep sense of
personal bereavement among all the
people and an abounding loyalty to
his memory. Rising, however, well
above these sentiments, and dominating them, were a spiritual temper in
the people, a religious enthusiasm, and
a consecration to Christ. Through
his episcopate Massachusetts had been

lifted Godward. This, it seems to me, was the climax of his powers, the finest illustration of his lifelong character, — that of turning men from himself to Christ, from the preacher to the Master. During his life he received such adulation as has been the lot of few men; and since his death he has been held in tender memory by thousands. His name is still heard in the homes, the colleges, the jails, and hospitals; but whenever his name is spoken, whenever his figure comes to memory, there is always in the background, uplifted, dominant and living, the form and spirit of his Master, Christ; the eye and thought instinctively turn from one to the other.

Through the pure and simple character of Phillips Brooks we look steadfastly into the infinitely richer, purer, and more glorious character, his Master, Jesus Christ.

The Riverside Press
Electrotyped and *printed by H. O. Houghton & Co.*
Cambridge, Mass., U. S. A.